All Families

LGBTQ+ Families

by Jen Breach

FOCUS
READERS.

BEACON

www.focusreaders.com

Focus Readers is distributed by North Star Editions:
sales@northstareditions.com | 888-417-0195

Produced for Focus Readers by Red Line Editorial.

Photographs ©: Shutterstock Images, cover, 1, 4, 6, 11, 14–15 (background, person wearing tank top, people wearing skirts), 15 (doctors), 15 (person in mirror), 15 (person wearing sweater-vest), 15 (person looking at phone), 15 (people in lower right wearing blue and green), 15 (person wearing star shirt, person wearing green striped t-shirt), 16, 22, 25, 29; iStockphoto, 8, 12, 19, 21, 27

Library of Congress Cataloging-in-Publication Data
Names: Breach, Jen, author.
Title: LGBTQ+ families / by Jen Breach.
Description: Lake Elmo, MN : Focus Readers, [2023] | Series: All families |
    Includes index. | Audience: Grades 2-3
Identifiers: LCCN 2022035396 (print) | LCCN 2022035397 (ebook) | ISBN
    9781637394595 (hardcover) | ISBN 9781637394960 (paperback) | ISBN
    9781637395684 (pdf) | ISBN 9781637395332 (ebook)
Subjects: LCSH: Sexual minorities' families. | Sexual minorities--Family
    relationships.
Classification: LCC HQ73 .B69 2023 (print) | LCC HQ73 (ebook) | DDC
    306.85086/6--dc23/eng/20220805
LC record available at https://lccn.loc.gov/2022035396
LC ebook record available at https://lccn.loc.gov/2022035397

Printed in the United States of America
Mankato, MN
012023

About the Author

Jen Breach (they/them) grew up queer and nonbinary in an otherwise cishet family of three big brothers, two parents, and one pet duck. Jen has worked as a bagel-baker, a code-breaker, a ticket-taker, and a trouble-maker. They now work as a writer, the best job ever, in Philadelphia, Pennsylvania.

Table of Contents

Chapter 1

Family Pride

Every June, many families take part in Pride Month. Pride is a celebration of **LGBTQ+ culture**. Some families go to Pride parades. One family might walk in the parade. They may carry a banner.

People display a rainbow flag during a Pride parade in Toronto, Ontario.

 Two million or more kids in the United States are being raised by at least one LGBTQ+ parent.

Another family may wave rainbow flags. Some families watch from the sidewalk. Others dance and sing at a concert.

During Pride Month, the whole LGBTQ+ community comes together. They form one very big family. Everyone is welcome to come as they are. Bright colors are everywhere. It's a joyful celebration of LGBTQ+ life, community, and families!

Did You Know?

In 2019, the New York City Pride parade set a record. Five million people marched.

Chapter 2

A Rainbow of Families

LGBTQ+ families are made up in many ways. They might have LGBTQ+ children. They might have LGBTQ+ parents. Or they might have both. Most LGBTQ+ families include **cishet** people, too.

 In the United States, up to 10 percent of adults are LGBTQ+.

LGBTQ+ families may be **biological families**. They can also be blended families. These families have children from earlier relationships.

LGBTQ+ parents are much more likely than other parents to adopt or foster. Adopting means adults become parents to a child who has other birth parents. Fostering is similar to adopting. But it is usually for less than two years.

For this reason, LGBTQ+ families are often different in another way.

More young people are identifying as genders that are not cis-male or cis-female, such as nonbinary.

They are more likely to include people of different races, national **identities**, or cultures.

LGBTQ+ families also have much in common with other families. Some LGBTQ+ parents are married.

 In the United States, approximately 30 percent of LGBTQ+ adults are raising children.

Others are not. Some LGBTQ+ parents live together. Others are separated or **divorced**. Still others are single parents. Children in

LGBTQ+ families might live in one household. Or they might be part of more than one.

LGBTQ+ families live in all kinds of communities. They live all around the world. For many years, the number of LGBTQ+ families has been rising. And it is likely to keep growing.

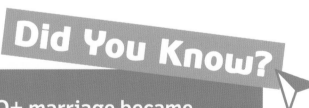

Did You Know?

In 2015, LGBTQ+ marriage became legal in all 50 US states.

All the Ways to Be

The term LGBTQ+ covers many types of identity. Identities play out in lots of ways. Gender identity is one. This is how someone sees their own gender. Pronouns are often important. Pronouns include he, him, she, her, they, and them. Some people use other pronouns, too. Or they use a combination.

Gender expression is how people show their gender. It can include how people act. It can also include how people dress.

Doctors assign genders for newborns. And people often assume others are certain genders. But these labels do not always match people's gender identities.

Ways of Thinking About Gender

GENDER BELIEF
How Others See Your Gender

GENDER IDENTITY
How You See Yourself

GENDER ASSIGNED AT BIRTH
What Doctors Assign

GENDER EXPRESSION
How You Show Your Gender

Chapter 3

A Rainbow Behind the Clouds

LGBTQ+ families can face many challenges. One might be **coming out** as LGBTQ+. Coming out is a personal action. It lets an LGBTQ+ person live as their true self. But coming out is not always easy.

Some people come out as LGBTQ+ when they are adults. Others come out when they are much younger.

Many LGBTQ+ people face homophobia. This is mistreatment because of someone's sexuality. LGBTQ+ people can also face transphobia. This is another type of mistreatment. It happens because someone is not cisgender.

This unfair treatment does not always look like hate. Sometimes people are just uncomfortable. But it's still **discrimination**. As a result, many LGBTQ+ people "pass" as cishet. Passing is when an LGBTQ+

Trans people of color face especially high rates of transphobia.

person lets someone think they are cishet. Sometimes they even pass within their family.

Being "out" can be a struggle as well. Strangers can misgender LGBTQ+ people. Strangers may think they are cishet. That can hurt.

Also, bullies may target LGBTQ+ children. Cishet children who are in an LGBTQ+ family can be targets, too.

Some challenges happen within LGBTQ+ families. Most LGBTQ+ families include both cishet and LGBTQ+ members. Sometimes they do not understand one another.

Did You Know?

LGBTQ+ high school students are twice as likely to be bullied as cishet students.

 Many LGBTQ+ students are bullied both in person and online.

LGBTQ+ people are not always accepted by their biological families. But some people join new families who accept them.

I LOVE
MY
LGBTQ CHILD

TORONTO PFLAG

PFLAG ❤ CANADA
Inspire change...pour le mie

Chapter 4

Bright Blue Skies

By the early 2020s, LGBTQ+ people had more rights than ever. But many people still faced discrimination. People can help fight this discrimination. Some of this work depends on allies.

 Groups such as **PFLAG** work with cishet people. They teach how to be allies to LGBTQ+ people.

Allies are cishet people who support LGBTQ+ rights.

Many groups support LGBTQ+ families. Some work in cishet communities. They work toward LGBTQ+ acceptance. For example, some groups talk to people who make books, movies, and TV. They

Did You Know?

The 1972 New York City Pride parade made history. Jeanne Manford marched with her gay son during the parade. She was the first ally to march.

 Using correct pronouns can help make all people feel welcome.

want media to show more LGBTQ+ people. They also want LGBTQ+ people to be shown positively.

Many schools and communities are helping, too. They make safe spaces for LGBTQ+ people. They encourage using correct pronouns.

They also celebrate diversity. That means welcoming people from a wide range of backgrounds and identities.

Schools can make groups for students. For instance, many schools have Gender and Sexuality Alliances (GSAs). In GSAs, LGBTQ+ students and allies work together. They work for more LGBTQ+ **visibility**, safety, and acceptance.

Families can also help. They can challenge discrimination in their

In places that are more supportive of LGBTQ+ people, LGBTQ+ families are better able to thrive.

own families. They can challenge it in other families, too. Groups might work with these families. They can help cishet people be better LGBTQ+ allies.

FOCUS ON
LGBTQ+ Families

Write your answers on a separate piece of paper.

1. How are LGBTQ+ families different from cishet families? How are they the same?

2. How could your school better support students in LGBTQ+ families?

3. When was LGBTQ+ marriage first legal in all 50 US states?
   - A. 1972
   - B. 2015
   - C. 2019

4. Why might some LGBTQ+ people choose to "pass"?
   - A. Passing is a true way for them to live.
   - B. Passing helps them come out.
   - C. Passing might help them avoid discrimination.

5. What does **misgender** mean in this book?

*Strangers can **misgender** LGBTQ+ people. Strangers may think they are cishet.*

    A. label someone with a wrong gender identity

    B. work against LGBTQ+ discrimination

    C. become someone's friend

6. What does **media** mean in this book?

*For example, some groups talk to people who make books, movies, and TV. They want **media** to show more LGBTQ+ people.*

    A. parents

    B. groups that work on causes

    C. types of art

Answer key on page 32.

Glossary

biological families
Families whose members are related to one another.

cishet
"Cis" means cisgender, or people who have the same gender as the one that doctors assigned at birth. "Het" means heterosexual, or people who are attracted to people of the opposite gender.

coming out
The ongoing process of a person making their LGBTQ+ identity known to others.

culture
A group of people and how they live, such as customs and beliefs.

discrimination
Unfair treatment of others due to who they are or how they look.

divorced
No longer married.

identities
The traits, labels, and beliefs that people define themselves with.

LGBTQ+
Letters that stand for lesbian, gay, bisexual, trans, and queer. The "+" stands for the many other non-cishet identities.

visibility
Being seen and understood in society and media.

To Learn More

BOOKS

Braun, Eric. *The Gay Rights Movement.* Minneapolis: Lerner Publications, 2019.

Felix, Rebecca. *#Pride: Championing LGBTQ Rights.* Minneapolis: Abdo Publishing, 2020.

Simon, Rachel E. *The Every Body Book: The LGBTQ+ Inclusive Guide for Kids About Sex, Gender, Bodies, and Families.* Philadelphia: Jessica Kingsley Publishers, 2020.

NOTE TO EDUCATORS

Visit **www.focusreaders.com** to find lesson plans, activities, links, and other resources related to this title.

Index

Answer Key: 1. Answers will vary; **2.** Answers will vary; **3.** B; **4.** C; **5.** A; **6.** C